THE UPS AND DOWNS AND UPS OF BUYING A HOLIDAY HOME ABROAD

RICHARD WALL

Copyright

Dedication

For Anita, Jo and Georgia

Contents

1 - Sod It

"Sod it, I'll buy it!"

I said this to myself while sitting in the estates agent's car, being driven back to his office.

Buy what?

I wasn't sure.

I had just seen a small house in a hamlet called l'Audibertie in the Dordogne in the 24th Département of France. 'Seen' had consisted of arriving in near-complete darkness with the house silhouetted black against a very dark grey night sky in October 1972. The totally black interior was opened up with the aid of the light of a cigarette lighter first locating the hole for the agent's key and then the same light source locating and setting fire to some screwed up newspapers that littered the floor.

"Two good rooms and a fine fireplace," said the estate agent, "and a fine staircase up to the roof space." These fine features were seen through the dancing shadows produced by the short-lived fiery torch – a situation that must have been not too dissimilar to that experienced by our cave-dwelling ancestors. All totally ridiculous as I hadn't seen or taken anything in, but the decision to buy was made when I had carefully, but very quickly, considered the expense of return trips to view further properties.

Back in Monsieur Rousillon's office, I signed what seemed to be endless pieces of paper by the seemingly delighted estate agent staff who must have been relieved to have sold this property, probably having had it on their books for years.

The sales team members, now amongst others, consisted of the agent and his interpreter who I learnt had worked as a second-hand car salesman at Vauxhall Bridge Road, in London, from a garage which is now long gone. I'm sure this must have been the garage that a year or so earlier I had very irritably visited, in a non-air-conditioned car on a stinking hot day, with a view to purchasing a sought-after car. I was told that they had never had one in stock and then that they had just sold it. Obviously a 'come on'.

Not a very reassuring start to virtually spending all my meagre savings.

* * *

That evening I stayed in the Hotel du Commerce, in Ribérac, where I enjoyed a good evening meal which included a starter, never before or since experienced, served in a ramekin, with a name ending in à la dieppoise which meant it deliciously contained seafood.

Ribérac, some five miles from l'Audibertie also contained M. Rousillon's office as well as all the facilities one required for life. Ribérac is a very pleasant and honest market town on the convergence of five roads deep in the northern part of the Dordogne, again, deep in rural France skirted by the delightful River Dronne.

After a good sleep, I awoke wondering what the hell I had signed up to buy.

I had arrived in Ribérac via Norfolk where I had been priced out of my long-dreamt-of holiday home due to a very quick price rise on suitable properties of around £1,000 on each of my few visits.

I then learnt of Ribérac from an article in a Sunday newspaper which centred on this patch of France where Brits were buying up holiday homes at very advantageous prices. A reccy visit during a camping holiday in the relatively nearby Medoc region, around 1970, confirmed this and gave me a great liking for this gentle, rolling rural area. A further year past then found me last in a queue of Brits – yes a queue – in M. Rousillon's Ribérac bureau with me requesting the smallest, cheapest house they had. Well over an hour had passed in that queue – hence, the fast-coming night when we set out to view the very place they thought I was looking for.

* * *

The hire car I had arrived in from Bordeaux Airport took me back to l'Audibertie where from the directions given to me by the agent I located the house. Before I could open the door with the key I now held, I was besieged by a seemingly large number of native l'Audibertians of all ages who seemed to mysteriously appear from all directions. My failed O-level French allowed me to understand their need to know how much I paid – or was it the rubbing of their index fingers and thumbs together? "Twenty-thousand old French francs," was my reply, which seemed to please them as I assumed that meant all their properties were worth far more.

Eventually, entering my new acquisition revealed that it did indeed consist of two ground-floor rooms each with a shuttered window, one with a fine large fireplace and a white glazed Belfast-type sink. The other had a walnut staircase hidden immediately behind a door which rose unevenly, and frighteningly creakingly, to a roof space which was heavily encroached upon by two poplar roof trusses. The space was lit by a gap on the two long sides at the eaves, three small, rectangular, unglazed openings together with a few slipped pantiles which allowed beams of morning sunlight to strike the uneven and ancient twisted floorboards. The roof space was very well-ventilated confirming it was originally a farmhouse with this space being used to store grain and other foodstuffs.

There was also, I discovered, a previously unmentioned cellar which one stepped down into from the side road that dropped down around the northern end of the house. According to the agent I had bought it from a gendarme, the last incumbent – so presumably it had not been part of a farm for some time, with any ancillary buildings being sold off in the past.

No bathroom, toilet or mains water, but there was evidence of mains electricity. All very basic, dirty and definitely fast falling into the class of derelict, but it fully fulfilled my request, made the previous day in his office, for the cheapest small cottage they had.

Water, I discovered, was drawn from a well immediately adjacent to the front door.

A full structural survey was completed in a couple of minutes – no visible internal or external wall cracks.

The deed was done, a humble holiday home purchased.

Back to Blighty and report to the family.

Back in Blighty, the report was not greeted with too much enthusiasm and summed up by a comment from the Mrs: "Well it's your money."

Hey ho! I suppose I did not expect much more.

* * *

I seem to recall that many more papers were posted to me for signing and returning and eventually the monies were paid over to the appointed French notaire. I dimly recall that the complete total paid was a tad under £2,000.

A formidable and very successful solicitor client, when learning of my purchase, inquired as to who had overseen the sale on my behalf was horrified at learning ... nobody. He explained that amongst all the papers I had blindly signed, I could have given my wife and children over to the slave trade or even worse. Fortunately (very fortunately), all proved kosher.

My wife, Anita (pregnant with Georgia at that time) and three-year-old Joanne were not the first to use 'Les Quatre Murs', as it cleverly became named. It was in fact Anita's sister, Marilyn, with her then boyfriend. This was followed shortly after by Jeremy, a younger work colleague of mine, and his fiancée. Between them, they very thankfully cleaned the place out, including a dead snake from the roof-space, and made it 'habitable'. They also sussed out the surrounding areas and, more importantly, made friends with the locals – in particular, with our immediate farmer neighbour, the formidable Madame Rene Gerbeaud.

* * *

Our first visit as a holiday came a year later when my daughter Georgia was six months' old.

Difficult to describe the initial shock Anita must have felt with the prospect of having to settle in for three weeks into such squalid conditions, let alone with such a young child. She remained silent for a full two hours but somehow we cleaned, deloused and debugged the place with the aid of Jeyes Fluid and Maws of Barnet's sterilisation liquid, both of which played a large part in the process. This was the period when the term 'The Hovel' was first used.

Somehow beds were already in place – probably donated by Madame Gerbeaud to the previous visitors. They joined a cot that somehow fitted into, or more likely onto, our car, along with a folding camping table and a couple of folding chairs which in turn joined a bench that had been cobbled together out of concrete building blocks and a well-worn timber plank by our previous visitors. There was the original white, glazed, ceramic, Belfast-type sink which discharged directly into the shallow ditch that bordered and ran alongside the High Street immediately in front of the cottage. Electric power was provided by throwing the mains control switch. Water was available 24 hours a day via the galvanised bucket when the lowered into the deep well by means of a chain and pulley. Sanitary facilities were provided by the Elsan Company and one of their bucket toilets which travelled down with us together with a camping double-ringed gas stove. In fact, this was all that was needed for a low-end very rough holiday.

2 - Travelling Down

The car journey down each year from St Albans became easier. The first trips were a nightmare in comparison to the later years. Initially, it took four hours to get to Dover for the ferry crossing which was eventually halved as the M25 and Q.E. Bridge were opened up. The boat crossing was always enjoyable, if often crowded.

On one occasion, we had not booked and on arrival at the ferry terminal were checked for our tickets.

"We've not got them yet."

"Blimey this is the busiest weekend of the year. The schools have just broken up. Get your tickets and join the queue over there. But you'll be lucky to get across this weekend."

What a start.

Tickets were obtained and the queue joined, but we were on board within 15 minutes. It became apparent that for every fully-booked ferry, there were a number of 'no-shows' due to punctures, breakdowns, etc. and those in the non-bookers' queue were allowed to take their place. We had stumbled on some very good luck. Once across the Channel, it was impossible to travel more than 20 to 25 miles in an hour – unless we were on the road between 12 noon and 2 pm when 30 to 40 miles were achieved. The French lunch is sacrosanct and roads more or less emptied during lunchtime. We had lunched on the ferry.

In the early days, one huge bugbear on French roads in August, was the bloody caravans which for some reason always seemed to travel in pairs, making it virtually impossible to get past for miles. I'm sure they were friends and were in touch with two-way radios. I can imagine the jist of their conversations: "We've got a nice queue building up behind Nigel, so slow down a bit more and we'll double its size before we get to the next town. I think we've got that English git we had last year. You know, the one screaming blue murder when he eventually got past."

* * *

The French motorway system was getting underway and, eventually, lengths of new dual carriageway were constructed and opened up, allowing bursts of speed. These, slowly over the years, became linked up into motorways and times for the 400-mile remaining French leg of the journey were slashed.

An overnight stop and meal were always on the schedule in a town that arrived around 5.30 pm on the Saturday. A hotel was always found immediately even though it was usually in August. On one occasion, we tried non-stop driving through the night. Just the once. It took me several days to get over it.

Each year I took to approaching the house, on arrival, from the Festalemps road to view the roof from a more elevated viewpoint. I yearly expected to find at least a partial collapse – which would have meant a hotel – but every year it was thankfully intact

* * *

We always planned to arrive on the Sunday afternoon so that we could clean out and be ready for an evening meal in one of the local eateries.

The best, but unfortunately the most expensive, mode of travel was the French Motorail from Calais to Brive. In later years this brilliant method was used twice – starting on the Saturday evening, sleeping overnight and arriving at Brive around 6.00 am on Sunday morning. Breakfast of coffee and croissant on the station's platform while the cars were being unloaded and then the drive to l'Audibertie to arrive around 9.30 am.

This allowed the house to be debugged and swept out by midday ready for lunch.

That's the way to do it!

3 - Out and About

Unpacking the car was carried out by Anita and myself as Jo and Georgia would immediately, on arrival, run off to discover who else was 'in town'. They would eventually return when the unpacking was finished with the full news. The 'whatsits'and the 'doodahs' are here, but not at home. The other 'whatsits' haven't arrived yet and so on. The object of searching out the prior-arrivals were their children who, with ours, constituted The Kids' Gang which did what all kids' gangs do.

The Hovel was soon swept out and de-cobwebbed and on one occasion a sleeping bat was disturbed and freed from the second room along with its accumulated droppings. Windows and their shutters were opened in each room and the entrance and the linking door were left open to allow fresh air to circulate. Hundreds of dead fly carcasses that had collected on the internal window frames were also removed.

Slowly, over the next few days, the place was made passably habitable.

When Georgia was old enough to leave her cot, Jo graciously allocated her new bed space in the most undesirable spot in their room – in the alcove of the still cobweb-festooned underside of the rising staircase.

* * *

One year, after the sweep-out, we went down to the nearby lake (Le Grand Etang) at La Jemaye, to eat at one of the food shacks that had evolved over decades only to find groups of eerily silent people standing in the twilight amongst the pine trees looking out at the lake. A black rubber Zodiac crewed by Pompadours and two wet-suited divers were some 50 yards out, obviously looking for something. We soon learnt that something was a boy who had gone missing that afternoon. We stayed until the search was given up when near-darkness fell. The boy's body was found early next morning when the search was renewed. A sad, very tragic and sobering experience.

* * *

A later occupation I never tired of while often relaxing at the lake was watching the first-time windsurfers trying to learn how to surf. It seemed to me they spent their time climbing up on-board, standing upright, and then falling off time after time. This went on for the whole hour of their hire period without moving more than a foot at a time. I cannot believe they enjoyed their efforts as much as I did!

Our own initial adventure on the water involved hiring a pedal boat which shortly after boarding took on water and then slowly listed to starboard sufficiently for the cry, "Abandon ship!" to be yelled.

After that alarming experience, we purchased a Li-lo on which Anita and the girls floated – which I'm told I took great delight in swimming quietly up behind and tipping the incumbents off. What larks girls, what larks!

* * *

The sandy surrounding soil below the pines and around the lake, in the autumn season, sported an unbelievably majestic display of fungi. Brown, yellow, red, blue, pink, white, orange and all the colours in between, in all sizes and shapes, which sprung up seemingly overnight. Their sight was truly magical.

Anyone knowing their mushrooms would have days of feasting.

* * *

L'Audibertie itself is a small farming hamlet consisting of a dozen or so farmhouses and their accompanying barns, many of which when we first arrived were vacant and up for sale. The whole area over several centuries had been carved out of La Forêt de la Double which sits on the very western side of the Massif Central just where the terrain starts to get gently lumpy. In each of the gentle folds, a stream occurs that eventually runs into the River Dronne and then in turn into the River L'Isle and finally into the mighty Dordogne. Large areas of the forest still exist in which oak, walnut, pine and sweet chestnut happily grow in the sandy/chalky soil. I understand that a few centuries ago, the whole wooded area was a wild malaria-infested swamp which was eventually drained by local monks when they established an efficient drainage system to reduce the boggy marshes. The forest flourished and became a safe refuge during the 100 Years' War (ironically from the English) and the Second World War. The forest also provided timber and charcoal via the local flat-bottomed sailing barges which plied their trade from nearby Aubeterre down the Dronne to Bordeaux, Bergerac and beyond. This trade has now vanished but the barges can still be seen in Bergerac – not trading wood products, but plying trips to tourists along the river Dordogne.

The splendid clear-water, fish-filled river Dronne starts in the Central Massif then flows westwards to Ribérac when it turns leftish to flow southwards, eventually to join the Dordogne. The forested areas that have been cleared are now farmed in pleasantly smallish-sized fields which support some animals but mainly arable crops which champion corn, cob corn and the ubiquitous mighty sunflower. The seeds of these sunflowers formed a large part of the Kids' Gang snacks when they were out doing their things. Steal a large head, break it up amongst the members present, take an individual fresh ripe seed and nip off the blunt end of the black casing with front teeth, squeeze the remaining casing between forefinger and thumb and the nutritious cornel will pop out – ready for eating. Thousands must have been devoured this way during their meet-ups.

Local features include the aforementioned lake, Le Grand Etang, a campsite with a small, supervised swimming area actually in the superb River Dronne at Aubeterre and, of course, the nearby very pleasant town of Ribérac. We soon learnt that Fridays were Ribérac's market days which, when we first arrived, was a relatively local affair with farmers selling their excellent produce in one half of the town's square, with the other half selling household goods from travelling traders who 'did' other town's markets on other days of the week. The market covered everything from cabbages to sealing wax but the most memorable items were the local produce of superb-looking vegetables, cheeses, pates, cut flowers, saucissons, fruit etc. Of these, the most splendid were the displays of the large, vibrant red tomatoes which took on a luminous glow in the strong sun.

A long-forgotten essential item were fly-papers which were readily available in the market. These ribbon strips of sticky paper when hung from, say, a central light-fitting proved a permanent resting place for flies.

Over the years, the size of the market grew like topsy and took over most of the central area, with traders spilling out into the surrounding streets and then eventually onto the main road through the town. At least one Friday a holiday became 'market day' for us when we would pick up items in an attempt to turn The Hovel into a luxury home: like a plastic bowl, a dust pan and brush or even a broom. Like every market day anywhere in the world it gave the opportunity for the locals to meet up and catch up on the news, chew the cud and enjoy a bevvy or two or three. A most worthwhile institution.

In our early days, I seem to recall, Ribérac supported two butchers and two wet fish shops where their fine produce was sold to supportive locals. The butchers memorably sold distinctively tasty steak hachets which were beefburger-style pats of minced meat obtained from the trimmings the butcher cut from the meat sold over the counter. These, together with their meurgez sausages, provided regular alternative dinners on the times we ate in.

Inevitably, the supermarkets arrived which reduced the fish and butchers to one a piece, and then they disappeared completely which helped tear the central heart out of the town, as they have very sadly succeeded in doing worldwide.

* * *

Slowly but surely as the years passed, everything started to fall into place: the journey time was halved as the new legs of dual carriageway were joined to form the RN10 motorway, leaving only a pleasant short section of the original A-class road from Angouleme to be negotiated on into Ribérac.

New places were found to eat and new places to regularly visit were discovered – amongst which was the truly delightful town Brantôme, which sat astride the river Dronne which then flowed gently (in summer anyway) and clearly and trout-filled down to Ribérac and beyond.

Aubeterre, another delightful town, was frequently visited to enjoy a coffee and cake in the tree-shaded little town square. Aubeterre sits on top of a steep hill on the other valley side of the Dronne and consequently resides in the neighbouring Département of the Charente. It also boasts an extraordinary monolithic church created in a cave in the side of the hill. It was during one of these coffee breaks in Aubeterre that Georgia, around the age of sixish, decided she was going to buy herself an ice cream. Off she went into a shop across the square and came out with an ice cream. I'm sure I would not have had the confidence at her age to have done that – let alone in a foreign country.

Saint-Émilion, another delight, was set on another hill overlooking the River Dordogne itself and surrounded by an ocean of vineyards, some of which produce the very best and prohibitively expensive claret wines. This was another great town to visit, but as the years passed it was noticeably getting visited by more and more tourists and became a real honeypot which, unfortunately, for me just took the edge off it. Like Brantôme, these towns were well worth yearly visits as was the local city of Perigieux with its multi-domed cathedral echoing those of the Sacré Cœur in Paris and even the main church in Ribérac. Perigieux also boasts an excellent market where those incredible fungi, truffles, are available – when in season.

4 - Madame Rene Gerbeaud

Before we, as a family, arrived the area was being Briticised to such an extent that one of the French TV companies sent a team to investigate the invasion for an item to include on their early-evening magazine programme. On asking around for proof, they were directed to l'Audibertie, which by then had a decent concentration of Brits. Apparently, on arrival, they were more than rewarded when they found Jeremy and his fiancée enjoying their holiday. So, with all the panache of a crack investigatory team, they put a bowler hat on him and gave him a furled umbrella and filmed him walking down the High Street. The result was shown nationally on French TV without so much as a royalty being paid to anyone.

* * *

We were the first Brits to buy in l'Audibertie, but by the time we arrived for our first holiday at least five other properties had fallen in the invasion. It was fast becoming a holiday village.

It was difficult to know how the locals felt about an invasion each summer of middle-class foreigners. On the face of it, they welcomed us most warmly and there was never any sign of animosity – in fact, the opposite. The income brought into the area must have been, and probably still is, substantial and is probably only partly responsible for the goodwill shown. This is in direct of opposition to some of the animosity shown to the immigrants in the UK who, amongst other things, in general, were perceived as taking money out.

There was rumoured to be some animosity or tensions between the l'Audibertians themselves – which probably must be the same in every small community throughout the world, which will have fermented over countless decades between people and, in turn, their families. This tribalism affected us in a very small way insomuch as we bought our eggs solely from Madame Gerbeaud which put us firmly into her camp. On arrival each year she would give me five cheek kisses. In French cheek-kissing etiquette I'm not sure what five meant but they were always a joy to receive and always formed part of our yearly arrival. Also, part of our arrival was the lovely smell of the crushed wild mint I had just driven over when eventually parking the car after two days on the road.

* * *

Madame Gerbeaud was the formidable farmer who lived in the neighbouring farmhouse whose yard had the blank rear wall of our hovel forming one of its sides. The yard itself was packed with bits and pieces of everything ever found in a farmyard: some bits in regular use, with many others kept for their future but never-occurring usefulness. The yard was patrolled by the friendly family farm dog that, if allowed, would have licked us to death. Another side of the yard was the cattle barn whose interior was festooned with ancient, dust-encrusted massive hanging and draped cobwebs which utterly and completely outdid any of Lady Faversham's Great Expectations' filmsets.

Mme. Gerbeaud farmed a number of fields, some of which were really quite small or miniscule when compared to the massive 'agri-fields' of northern France. These were no doubt the result of the Napoleonic Code regarding the inheritance of land having to be split evenly between siblings on the death of the owner. This may well be worth checking out with experts for people wishing to buy property in France with a view to an inheritance.

M.Gerbeaud, though, was a diminutive little man who we saw twice daily drawing a pail of water from our well. This, he did 365 days a year which was an absolute blessing as it kept the water 'sweet'. Unfortunately, he was not averse to a glass or two or three, which limited his usual abilities, which in turn resulted in bouts of shouting rage from Madame which, I reckon, could be heard on calm days in Dover.

Mme. Gerbeaud farmed diversely over a number of fields scattered around the area and, every morning, she took to one of them her half-dozen or so cattle to graze, and every evening brought them back. They went past every morning well before we arose but we were always aware that this had happened by the freshly dropped pats on the road. These pats sometimes strangely attracted up to six White Admiral butterflies who obviously enjoyed their moisture before the sun dried them out.

Talk about the beauties and the beast!

* * *

Every year, on a Sunday, we were invited to dinner with Mme. Gerbeaud which she prepared from scratch, or so it seemed, in no time at all. The meal started with a dressed green salad with hard-boiled egg slices, then half a Charentais melon each. The main course was a pot-roasted chicken or rabbit plus veg. Dessert was often a cherry clafutis, with the feast finishing with unbelievably sharp-tasting cherries pickled in her own homemade eau de vie. All superb in freshness and taste and prepared in seemingly minutes between visits to her fields. The rabbit or chicken being slaughtered and cleaned at the start of the meal's preparation. We – and certainly I – always thought it a minor miracle. If it were rabbit, we had to tell Georgia that it was chicken, for we had a pet rabbit at home and the thought of eating Miffy's French cousin was not on. We ate in a small, dark, all-purpose living room around an oblong central table, seated on benches either side, and alongside a perpetual fire above which hung the chain-suspended, lidded, black cast-iron roasting pot.

Apart from this all-purpose room, I was never sure what other accommodation was provided. Obviously, a bedroom, but I'm not sure it contained a bathroom and therefore a toilet. The great outdoors, I'm sure, provided this facility. A Belfast-type sink, washing bowl, a long case clock, TV and a storage unit filled most of the remaining space in the main room and all these were accompanied by the pail, sitting in the sink, which daily collected the water from our well.

It was always a huge contrast once the meal was finished and we stepped out into the blazing heat and a Mediterranean intensity of light which we rarely, if ever, enjoy in the UK. A period of R & R was necessary after such a dinner, but an evening meal was not.

Jo and Georgia were never great fans of this event as it cut deeply into gang time.

5 - The Frogs

We always considered Madame Jumas as the Grand Dame of l'Audibertie. She lived with her daughter Madame Casabon in the immediate neighbouring farmhouse up the High Street. They never appeared to farm and were consequently always well turned out. What farming they did was carried out by hired hands for whom she always cooked lunch. The smells from her kitchen of roasting meats were always a delight but, unfortunately, we were never invited to eat there – possibly because we bought our eggs from Madame Gerbeaud. Her great grandchild, Cyril, was in residence in August and he became another valued member of the kids' gang.

Further down the hill in the Moulin de l'Audibertie, M. Jean-Jacque Boudeaux self-built a family home aside a stream that ran into the Rizonne which ran into the Dronne which ran into the L'Isle etc. This stream teamed with damselflies and supplied water to a trout farm which had been incorporated into the house. Unfortunately, the farm never got into production during our residency. Now, M.Boudeaux was apparently a successful farmer who bought up a number of fields, and possibly small farms, as the original owners sold or died off. He eventually became Mayor of Festalemps which is the commune in which l'Audibertie nestles. His elder son was very active on the farm and enjoyed hurtling around the local roads on his tractor pulling a wildly bouncing large, flat-back trailer.

Another local resident was M.Dubois who also enjoyed a glass or three which eventually got him banned from driving when being caught over the limit. This did not stop him from visiting the local village bars as it appeared one did not require a licence to drive farm equipment on the roads – hence, his tractor became very active.

Madame Coco lived somewhat isolated down a nearby lane. She kept a flock of geese who, when you walked past her cottage would kick up the most unholy row and threaten to bite you to pieces if ever the intervening fence gave way. She also had a grandchild, Cecelia, staying with her for August and she also became a member of The Kids' Gang. This gang must have had an unpaid membership of twelve or so at its zenith.

* * *

Two elderly women would return home in upper l'Audibertie, often in the late afternoon, always fully dressed in black with large straw bonnets. They regularly walked past The Hovel carrying baskets of alfalfa, which, I assumed, was food for their chickens. They created a scene that must have been familiar for hundreds of years. Again, they were always so pleasant and polite with their greetings. Another remnant of a long-past era was seeing on that first day of purchase an ox-cart being drawn by an ox down the 'High Street'. I never saw that scene again. If both these events had been seen together they would of created a picture, apart from the road surface, that would have been commonplace possibly 300 or more years ago.

* * *

In past decades l'Audibertie boasted a school which Madame Casabon had actually attended. There was also a cobbler's shop which was unoccupied when we first arrived but was still recognisable by a faded painted boot above the entrance door. The property later became owned by another Frenchman who had the external walls rendered but thankfully left the boot untouched. A delightful reference to a bygone era.

Many years after our arrival, a ladies' hairdressing salon was opened in an old farmhouse in upper l'Audibertie. By the amount of extra cars passing The Hovel, it appeared to be very successful to the point where the High Street through the village, at times, resembled a mini M1.

Hairdressers – what next? A pizza parlour? A hamburger joint?

6 - Les Rossbifs

Now the Brits were a different lot all together. All middle-class and relatively comfortably off, if judged by the standard of renovations they had and were making to their farmhouses. This left us at the bottom of the pile in The Hovel. They came from all over the UK – Cheshire, St Albans, Arundel, Maidenhead, Lewes, Cambridge etc. All acceptable middle-class environs and amongst them was a poly' lecturer and publisher, a retired monk and now translator of foreign technical manuals, a doctor and his articled solicitor wife, a manufacturer of ceramic switches and insulators, and myself an architect. We also had a German architect, Rainer, who had built himself a separate self-contained two storey holiday home within a cavernous barn. An ingenious solution which I'm not sure I would have thought of.

As previously said, we were the first to buy but not to arrive, so that I can safely say all the others were johnny-come-latelys – but, nevertheless, we welcomed them all as the village elders.

Bring us your wealthy but pallid sun-seekers!

Their children were always ready joiners of the Kids' Gang which met as soon as possible after breakfast as their parents' activities would allow. Where and what they did was never revealed – but they sure seemed to enjoy themselves and many have remained friends well into their adulthood. One place in their adventures that was regularly mentioned was 'The Ghostly Farm'. Ghostly, because it was a completely vacant farm complex but locked up. The farmhouse featured a short length of steeply-pitched roof of the kind seen on grand châteaux. The whole deserted complex exuded status with an air of foreboding, not only to the gang but also to us adults who looked at it through its locked entrance gates.

In retrospect, it seems extraordinary that we had no qualms about allowing our four- and seven-year-old kids to disappear off to God-knows-where for hours on end with the gang which was led by, at best, a pre-teenager. Lunchtimes were often preceded by agitated parents striding down the High Street loudly imploring their offspring to return home immediately.

Recent interrogation revealed that the Kids' Gang spent their time just wandering and investigating vacant barns and buildings including the old cobblers and The Ghostly Farm itself. These activities were sustained by the intake of thousands of sunflower seeds.

* * *

People and families changed over the years and were replaced by others. One of these newcomers was a retired French customs officer from Le Havre. Yes, a Frenchman and his family, in the renovated farmhouse opposite ours. He was the only member of that family we got to know and he was forever telling us about Calvados – that is calvados 'pas commercial' (not shop bought). He therefore became known as 'Monsieur Calvados'. His wife seemed fixated with washing clothes in a washing machine she kept under cover of an overhanging roof outside their house. Now, constant wastewater from this seemingly continually-used contraption soaked into the surrounding earth via a septic tank which I'm sure was responsible for making our well water unpotable. I'm sure it was not the stopping of M. Gerbeaud drawing two pails of water every day simply because Mme. Gerbeaud had suffered a mild heart attack and was told to only drink mineral water from plastic bottles.

Oh no, it was that bloody washing machine!

A local laboratory test confirmed the presence of millions of microbes in our well and it was therefore unpotable, so it was plastic bottled water for drinking and boiled well water for tea for us.

Another family of newcomers had just returned from years in Kuala Lumpur and had bought a holiday home in l'Audibertie. Mr KL was, I think, a retired tea or rubber planter and was successful given the sums of money he was lavishing on his property which eventually gloried in new Velux roof windows as well as a swimming pool constructed in its spacious garden.

Times they were a changing.

It was at one of their evening soirées that I received what I considered a bollocking from another guest for not being able to hold a conversation in French but had nevertheless bought a house in France. She delighted in telling me that she enjoyed a chat over the gate with the locals. I explained that I had a wife and children who could more than fulfil that requirement leaving me to enjoy France without the chat of everyday country folk. A poor argument which I know I did not come out of too well. Never mind – as long as I can order a beer in French. Can't speak French – indeed! I should have told her about the time I went into a local village shop to buy some bread.

"Du pain s'il vous plaît, Madame," asked I, in my very best French.

"Pardon Monsieur?"

After being asked to repeat my simple request, a couple of times, the owner said, "Ah, oui," and retired to the back of her shop to return a moment later with a string of garlic. It's not me that can't speak French – it's the French.

Now, these two groups of diverse people, the locals and the Brits, came together each August in seemingly complete harmony and certainly with no overt animosity. It must be of interest to any sociologist that a totally rural hamlet of hundreds of years standing could be swamped by foreigners within a year and without any outward signs of friction surfacing.

One small incident that did threaten this amiable peace occurred between a French holiday home owner and an English one. They shared a common vehicular access and the French family, for ease of parking their car, minutely encroached upon land and – worst still – the lawn being cultivated by the English. So, there appeared one day a row of half a dozen or so stakes, each bearing a dual-nationality flag along the boundary between the two properties. The postcard-sized flags facing the English showed the French tricolor and the face facing the French showed the Union Jack.

Not the best way for promoting harmony amongst nations.

* * *

I initially felt concerned that The Hovel did not have any land attached to it but it was soon made apparent that this was, in fact, a blessing. Other Brits not-so-deprived were burdened with the yearly task of 'tidying up' which seemed to take up a large part of their holiday daylight time. The main culprit was their 'lawn' which by the time they arrived back in August each year resembled areas of 'set aside' with any surrounding shrubbery dramatically encroaching. Hours and hours of hard work in the summer heat were needed just to make their patches usable let alone presentable. The Hovel's minute patch, on the other hand, was totally neglected to become a wildlife sanctuary which allowed more time to enjoy the delights of the surrounding countryside, sights and local amenities – a situation that became apparent very quickly in the first year, and one that future holiday home owners might like to consider.

7 - Problems

Holiday lets for those who had suitable properties were an obvious source of income, but sometimes came with drawbacks. One such event involved Malcolm who lived near the southern limit of l'Audibertie, in a delightful holiday home which even contained a spiral staircase. He received, at home in the UK, a distressed phone call one Saturday from his newly-arrived 'lockateurs', as the hirers are called in France, complaining that all the sanitary appliances were not working as nothing was running or flushing away.

"Don't worry" I'll call my local handyman to sort it out."

Malcolm's call disclosed that it was a French national holiday, one of the many more than the UK enjoys, and that his handyman would not be returning until midweek. Quelle horreur! A true emergency. Only one way out of this if he was not to suffer a penalty which could easily be increased with the intervention of solicitors and their like – catch the Saturday-night ferry from Newhaven and drive through the night to personally rectify the problem. Arriving early on Sunday morning, he discovered the septic tank was bang full up and could take no more. Only one solution – start digging out the problem. So, up to his armpits, he nobly started digging. I don't know where the problem was cleared to, but all was operational again by Sunday afternoon. Just in time for a now-working shower and a grabbed meal before driving back to Blighty. Crossing again, this time by the Sunday-night ferry, he was able to attend his place of employment on Monday morning smelling sweetly, but totally shattered. What a way to spend a dirty weekend in France.

Another horror story occurred when a winter burst pipe in a Brit's property (the one that had served previously as the school) and was noticed by the locals, in early spring, to have water cascading out under the front door. They turned off the main external stopcock but the internal damage only became apparent when the first of the owners' lockateurs arrived to find the interior walls, furniture, bedding et al covered in black mildew. I understand a full refund was made. There were some things to be said for not being able to hire out a hovel.

* * *

A highly amusing incident occurred one warm still morning when I was enjoying a cup of coffee sitting on top of our low garden wall with my back against the well housing unintentionally, but unavoidably, listening to our newly-arrived neighbours discussing and compiling a shopping list for their forthcoming supermarket trip.

"Milk, butter, cheese, fruit ..." etc. Abruptly during its preparation, the husband broke in and said, "Oh I forgot to tell you I saw Mrs Robinson in Waitrose on Wednesday." There was a short but pregnant pause before the wife replied

"You're a fucking genius."

I collapsed immediately into laughter and had to run inside. I have no idea why she thought he was that kind of genius. I can only assume it was caused by his comment being in complete contrast and irrelevant to the job in hand, as was her totally unexpected reply – the cause of my merriment.

* * *

One event that was not so amusing was when Georgia became sick enough one year for us to take her to a doctor in Ribérac. He diagnosed dysentery which he thought she had probably picked up by swallowing the lake water from La Jemaye. The treatment he prescribed consisted of twice-daily injections of medication into her buttock. This, he carried out with military precision by clicking his heels, standing rigidly to attention, smartly saluting and then on each occasion repeating "Pour La Reine" and then gently lowering the needle into the required spot. Georgia took this whole procedure very stoically. This treatment was accompanied by a diet of boiled rice and carrots for the rest of our stay that year, which meant Georgia missed out on some memorable meals including one in Le Chabrol Restaurant in Brantôme which had then acquired a Michelin star. While we enjoyed these meals,

Georgia was babysat by a visiting lockateur while trying to enjoy her rice and carrots.

Not a great way to spend the best part of your holiday.

* * *

Another year, on arrival, we learnt of the tragic death of the vicar's wife. She was one of those blessed people who are able to walk into a room of strangers and immediately become the centre of interest by the sole dint of her personality. She had suffered a heart attack in their French house and had died mercifully quickly. She was a true loss to our little community.

The vicar, amongst other posts, had been the vicar of a parish in the East End of London. He was also the vicar on the Sunday night 'God Slot' on Radio Caroline the 1960s pirate pop radio station based on a ship, bobbing about in the North Sea, outside British territorial waters. He was large, very likeable and a great character and enjoyed single malt whisky which he generously shared with me on a couple of very enjoyable occasions. On leaving his house, on those occasions, he bade us farewell from his elevated, pulpit-like terrace by raising his arms high above his head, palms facing out and announcing, "Jesus loves you."

Unfortunately, later, we learnt that he had suffered a mini stroke but was fortuitously taken to hospital by the local taxi/ambulance service. The stroke was suffered on the first floor and the ambulance men wisely decided that he was too large to be taken down the narrow and unguarded staircase. Fortunately, the house had been built cut into the side of a hill, so that the first-floor rear bedroom window was conveniently at the standard height to the outside ground level. So, they took him out of the window with the stretcher and carried him around the side of the house down to the ambulance below. The stretcher was duly passed out with the first man now waiting outside, while the second man climbed out of the window to join him. For this manoeuvre to take place, the stretcher was laid to rest on the windowsill. That's when the screaming started. The ambulance men were unable to understand what the hell was the cause which continued for some time while rudimentary investigations took place. It was eventually decided that the best help for this patient was to get him into hospital as quickly as possible. The stretcher was lifted and immediately the cause was learnt. The vicar had been gripping the sides of the stretcher and his fingers of both hands were being crushed between the weighty stretcher and the stone windowsill. Fortunately, he made a good recovery but was advised by his consultant that whisky was 'out'. Again, fortunately, all was not lost as red wine was suggested as an alternative – so grain was replaced by the vine!

LES QUATRE MURS

PRAYING MANTIS

l'Audibertie, Dordogne.
GHOSTLY FARM
LES QUATRE MURS
TO VANXAINS
OLD COBBLERS
FARM ROAD
FARM TRACK
TO FESTALEMPS
OLD SCHOOL HOUSE
HIGH STREET
TO FESTALEMPS
FARM ROAD
FARM TRACK
N
100m
MINT

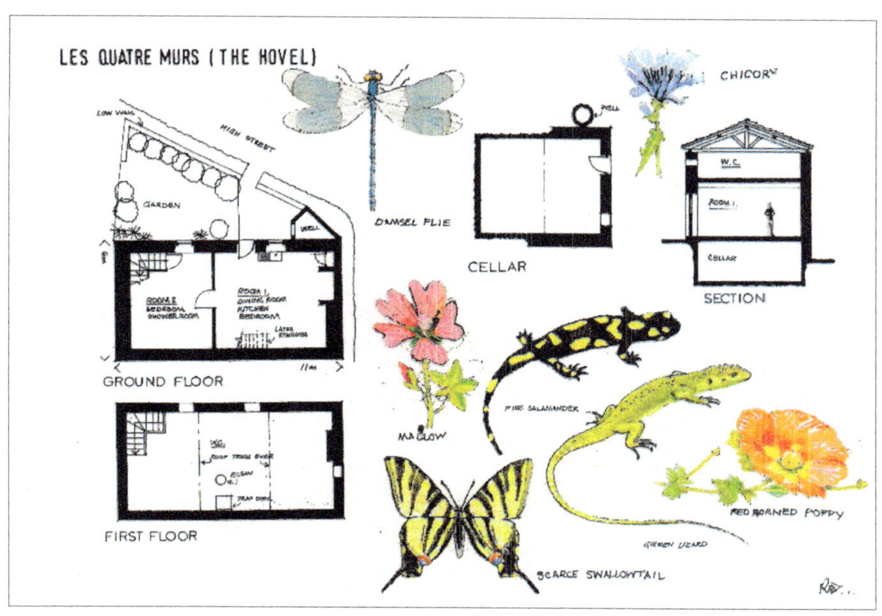
LES QUATRE MURS (THE HOVEL)
LOW WALL
HIGH STREET
GARDEN
WELL
ROOM 2 BEDROOM SHOWER ROOM
ROOM 1. DINING ROOM KITCHEN BEDROOM
GROUND FLOOR
FIRST FLOOR
DAMSEL FLIE
CELLAR
CHICORY
W.C.
ROOM 1.
CELLAR
SECTION
MALLOW
FIRE SALAMANDER
GREEN LIZARD
RED HORNED POPPY
SCARCE SWALLOWTAIL

GHOSTLY FARM

THE HIGH STREET
CHICORY
VIPER'S BUGLOSS
HAREBELL
LOOKING SOUTH.....
LES QUATRE MURS
aka The Hovel.
and LOOKING NORTH

ENVIRONS - l'Audibertie
FARM ROAD
WALNUT
SWEET CHESTNUT
FARM TRACK to FESTALEMPS
6/20

BRANTÔME
Le GRAND ETANG- La JEMAYE

Le MOULIN du ROC, Restaurant
YELLOW WATER LILLY
and BROWN TROUT
ENTRANCE
DINING TERRACE from across RIVER DRONNE
6/10

8 - The Throne

Even with all the continual improvements over the years, there remained one big bugbear to all this new-found luxury – it was the Elsan. Yours truly emptied this appliance twice a holiday and then, finally, again on the last day, giving it a good rinse out ready for next year's visit. Not a job I enjoyed at the best of times. The depository for its contents was the Commune's toilets at Festalemps in the shower building located at the entrance end of a decent-sized open-grassed area which served as the Commune's assembly area for their gatherings and Jour de Fetes. It may, in past eras, even possibly have been used for public guillotines. Anyway, it was secluded and I think we were the only people in the latter years to use the showers and even that stopped once we had installed ours. Proof of this was the lack of entries, apart from ours, in the cobwebbed, encrusted notebook which showerers were obliged to sign and place a small fee in the locked, metal-slotted money-box. In later years, our names were the only ones appearing. A sign, I suppose, that the local living standards were steadily improving, which I'm sure they were – and certainly a lot faster than ours!

The Elsan was gingerly transported in the back of the car, securely lidded and tied in an upright position in the hope that there was no spillage. Thankfully, there never was. The crunch came in the latter period of tenure. When arriving at the toilets, its entrance was virtually blocked by around twenty French people enjoying their evening alfresco barbequed meal seated on the grass. They had arrived earlier that day in 'gypsy' horse-drawn caravans on some sort of organised holiday deal which travelled the quiet lanes of rural France stopping at villages with suitable overnight sites. Undaunted, I embarrassingly pressed on with my necessary task by carefully stepping over and between the caravaners with many a "pardonez" and "excusez moi." I even stayed long enough to hose it out, making it presentable enough for the next year. This incident caused me great concern as I thought it was now going to be a regular yearly obstacle course while the 'gypsies' enjoyed their meals around the toilets. They did this even when there was more than ample open-grassed space available elsewhere – what is it with the French and toilets?

* * *

It was back home in the winter of that year that I came across an advert for an eco-toilet which reduced, it claimed, a fortnight's waste of a family of four into a brick-size piece of manure clean enough to be handled and which, when spread on the ground, turned that ground into a veritable clover patch. It seemed the answer to all my concerns.

Further research confirmed this and so, at huge expense – just short of the third of the cost of the hovel – it was purchased and duly arrived in a cardboard box which just fitted into the rear of the estate car. That next summer, I spent a considerable length of time installing it into the roof space. The

Elsan, while still in use, looked forlorn and undignified alongside this gleaming, cream, plastic interloper which really lived up to the name of a "throne" – electrical power connected, an earthing rod sunk and connected, and its ventilation flue connected and discharged through the eaves. The Elsan and was emptied and cleaned and, now redundant, placed in a far corner of the roof space. The new throne took its place majestically centre stage.

The throne was fully operational and taking its place in the yet again upgraded hovel. It was working as per manual: waste being dried and being mixed with the peat (initial supply supplied). We had definitely redefined the status of a hovel to that of a grand hovel.

Then it happened. On the night of the third day, a mighty Dordogne electrical storm broke with a monumental simultaneous thunderclap and lightning flash striking the metal pole which, attached to the hovel, carried our overhead mains power supply. The resultant electrical surge tripped our mains switch which was easily rectified by the pressing of a red button. However, the following morning it was discovered the throne had ceased working. Prodding and poking did not remedy the problem, so for the rest of our stay that year the Elsan was resurrected and placed alongside its failed replacement. On our return to be UK, and in discussion with the manufacturers, it was determined that the resultant electrical surge had buggered things and it needed a new whatsit. The whatsit came in the post and was fitted the following year. The motor came back to life but, because the waste/peat mixture had dried to an unmovable solid mass, its powerful motor stripped the teeth off the plastic cogs which turned the mixing paddles. Another year out of action. Later that year, replacement cogs arrived and in the following year it was discovered they did not fit. Another year out of action. The Elsan must have been feeling very smug. An attempt to contact the manufacturers on our return to Blighty revealed the company had gone out of business and no longer existed. Four bloody years from inception to total redundancy had lapsed and the old faithful had only three days out of employment. How she must have laughed at the throne – now, totally useless and which she now totally replaced.

The old simple ways are very often the best.

Just to complete the whole toilet fiasco, the 'gypsies' were never seen again.

* * *

Despite the toilet setback, the hovel was falling into place with improvements being made over the years with more bits and pieces being transported down. Among these bits were a second-hand electric kettle, pieces of wood to make things, a flat-pack chest of drawers and set of metal hanging rails complete with a variety of hangers. Eventually, a futon arrived, bringing with it more comfortable sitting and sleeping. A second-hand electric table-top fridge also made the journey which provided cold drinks and allowed food to be prolonged in its useful state. That was only when Anita, much to my chagrin, found it was never completely plugged in which was why it gave us very erratic cooling conditions for a couple of years.

The original alarming, creaking, walnut staircase was eventually made redundant by a new, very expensive, conventional timber staircase installed by a local well-respected builder. This rose from the living room to the first floor through a trapdoor to one of the most spacious toilets in Christendom. The toilet being the royal blue Elsan which stood majestically alone in the vast space – well, vast for an Elsan or any other make come to that. Washing facilities were provided by a Mme. Gerbeaud-donated ceramic washbowl and jug which sat upon the transported camping table in the second room – Jo and Georgia's bedroom.

* * *

After the toilet fiasco, the real piece de resistance came in later years when yours truly built a shower to sit alongside the washbasin. A submersible pump was lowered into the well to pump water into a storage tank now sharing the roof space with the Elsan. The level of the water in the tank was governed by a float switch. All piping was garden hose fixed with jubilee clips, and the showerhead was a garden watering rose and hose directly connected to the tank. The shower tray was a market-bought large plastic bowl positioned directly below the first-floor tank. Brilliant – a shower with water from the well. The only problem was that the water was evilish-cold even after standing in the heat of the roof-space for hours. So, to overcome this discomfort, I later fitted an immersion heater controlled by a pull switch which hung adjacent to the front door so that when we went out for the day, the switch was pulled and on our return the chill had been removed. A piece of work even Heath Robinson would have been proud of.

* * *

The Hovel was fast losing its lowly standing and becoming a one-star Hovel – we now had a heated shower, a sturdy staircase to the basic toilet, a futon, hanging rails and a chest of drawers. I even constructed a sturdy dining table made from timber bought locally, around which stood six bentwood dining chairs which were being sold by the thousand in all manner of local retail outlets from garages to hairdressers. They originated from North Africa, possibly Algeria, and sold at a price that could not be ignored. Decades later, I saw the same chairs being sold in a London Habitat store for many times the price, but even then they were a bargain at £20 each. Perfect for casual seating in any home county conservatory.

* * *

An eco-addition which any warrior would have been proud of, but never installed, was a solar-heated hose loop that would have been connected to the roof-space storage tank. But, as with many a plan of mice and men, the immersion heater was installed before this earth-saving idea got off the ground.

Talking of mice, we were inconvenienced one year by mice running around inside The Hovel and at night somehow getting onto the sink draining board and rattling the pots and plates in their search for food scraps. This was most disconcerting when attempting to get to sleep and I eventually discovered how they lowered themselves back onto the floor by jumping down the side of the sink. Below their launch site, I placed a pail of water in which they plunged where, squeaking, they swam around for a few seconds before they drowned. This overcame the problem but I now think this barbaric and I'm deeply ashamed that I had thought of such a method of curing the problem. The answer would have been to discover their entry hole (which was found a few days later) and to have blocked it up.

A country wood mouse had more of a right to be in L'Audibertie than I did.

9 - Flora, Fauna and Hail

While all these improvements and shenanigans were taking place, the Dordogne continued being the Dordogne. Farmers farmed, bakers baked, fields of corn grew as high as elephants' eyes and the ubiquitous fields of sunflowers flourished below the pounding sun they continually turned to.

We were woken every morning by the crowing of the local cocks and then serenaded by the cooing of the wood pigeons that had made their base in an ivy-covered stonewall opposite. As the morning heat rose, the cicadas joined the pigeons in what became the equivalent of the dawn chorus.

Although abundant, the wildlife was noticeably secretive, doubtless due to the French, certainly in rural areas, shooting everything that was edible during their hunting season. I did however catch sight of many a snake of various lengths, a small family of red deer, a Nightjar, countless lizards, young wild boar (in the car's headlights), a coypu and even a sighting of a rare, secretive French Robin. One group, however, was totally abundant. They were the Lepidoptera or butterflies. They were wonderfully everywhere in all colours, sizes and speeds. Some large dark-coloured jobs flew so fast and in such straight lines they were impossible to identify. They were obviously late for their daily meetings wherever those were – probably over the next hill range. Others more languid allowed identification such as the Swallowtails, the Admirals, the Tortoiseshells and all the common – but now, relatively scarce – species we are blessed with in the UK. The outstanding butterfly I saw turned out to be the Scarce Swallowtail which, when I first caught sight of it, in a sunny clearing in a wood, I swore was flying backwards – an extraordinary sight and experience; while the outstanding moth I saw was the daytime Hover Moth which fed, hovering hummingbird-like, with its tongue inserted into the flowers, searching out the pollen.

A wonderful experience occurred one day, again in the woods, when Georgia came running up to be asking me to "look at this". This was a Praying Mantis which had just landed on her jumper. Most children and, I'm sure, adults would have screamed blue murder, but she was savvy enough to know her father would have been interested in such a bizarre object. Praying Mantis in the Dordogne – I thought they only lived in places like the Sahara rainforests.

Another unique experience, for me, occurred when walking on a wet road out of l'Audibertie I caught sight of what I thought was a highly shiny, black and yellow plastic child's purse. I immediately thought how out of place and ugly it looked in such natural surroundings but as I neared, it turned out to be a living fire salamander which I then helped to the side of the road, hopefully to lose itself in the vegetation and cease to be an eyesore to the delicate senses of any other passer-by.

* * *

Flowers swarmed the sides of the lanes to such an extent I decided to log the more unusual ones. With the aid of my wildflower book, I got as far as wild carrot, viper's-bugloss, yellow and purple loosestrife, chicory, tree mallow, great mullein, common and purple toadflax, teasel, round-leafed fluellen, meadow clary, red-horned poppy and many, many more taken for granted and overlooked. A sawn-down plastic bottle acting as a vase carried a display of these Anita-gathered beauties in our fireplace throughout our stay.

My place as a botanist was confirmed when confronted with a small chalky outcrop, by the side of a road, I stated this was the exact habitat for harebells and then, much to my huge delight, right bang in the middle, was a lone one – magic.

Snails, hidden during the hot days, appeared in their thousands if it had rained during the evening when the locals came out with their buckets and torches to collect them. They, of course, were bound for cooking pots where, when combined with heat and the correct ingredients, they were transformed into splendid meals.

* * *

One morning, while taking a walk along the edge of a nearby wood, peacefully viewing the myriad of butterflies that were fluttering by, I was suddenly stopped in my tracks by the most unholy noise I've ever heard emanating from the other side of a bush. This noise cannot be described in words but all I know is that I was scared rigid and the hair on my arms and neck stood straight. The frightening, screaming, howling, guttural, grunting and shrieking thankfully abated and was then replaced by loud thumping noises on the ground followed by scampering noises through the undergrowth. I relaxed and thought it / they had gone. My first thought, from the thumping, was that it was a deer guarding its young but before I had taken another step that hideous noise started again. I turned and ran. I ran 200 metres in well under five seconds, and that is without the word of a lie or any exaggeration whatsoever. It was not until months later that I realised it must have been a male wild boar standing guard over its family which I had heard running from its perceived threat. I bet they were slower than I was in my flight from my real threat. In retrospect, I think

I was lucky not to have been gouged, possibly to death, by his tusks. I now have a great and huge respect for these animals and will only have any dealings with them if presented in small cooked pieces on a dinnerplate.

* * *

A natural phenomenon that could never be overlooked was the local night sky unsullied by light pollution – it was magnificent with stars the size of saucers. I realise that this must have been standard in the UK during the war-time blackouts. So many stars that it was difficult to pick out the common constellations that were visible even through our light-polluted skies at home. The almost-forgotten Milky Way was truly beautiful with Cygnus, the Swan, brightly flying down its path. Orion, Pleiades, Cassiopeia etc. were all in superb condition nestling amongst billions of their mates. The August meteor shower, occurring around 12 August, was always worth looking out for, with some years more spectacular than others.

One year, I transported my half-decent telescope down to take a closer look at things and what a joy that turned out to be. One super-bright 'star' I concentrated on appeared to be always out of focus – until I realised I was being confused by the rings of Saturn. A complete knockout!

* * *

Another natural phenomenon occurred, which stood out amongst all the others was that one evening, the temperature did not seem to drop and the twilight hours seemed extended into an unfamiliar grey-greenie sort of light.

All seemed different that evening and around 3 am we were woken by a loud, but totally unfamiliar, noise accompanied by howling wind. A small pane of glass was alarmingly smashed in the entrance door – all was not as it should be. On very cautiously venturing out of bed to see what the hell was happening, it became apparent it was caused by several billion golfball-sized, discus-shaped hailstones which had shattered the peace as well as many a tree, hedgerow, car roof and bonnet, windscreen – and even the Kuala Lumpur's new roof windows. Clay roof pantiles had also taking a bit of a battering. In the early morning light, peering outside onto the road, these hailstones appeared in ghostly heaped banks. Thankfully, the storm and the wind passed and the village gathered on the road in strangely cold conditions to discuss this unfamiliar event where we learnt of each other's small disasters. We later learnt that the storm had started a mile or so away and moved in a quarter-mile-wide path destructively over l'Audibertie and on into Ribérac, where shop awnings, left out overnight, were shredded. To all us Brits this this was a new experience, but to the locals it was not unfamiliar. Many a local grape harvest has been decimated over the years by these hailstorms. There were rumours of a horse left out in a field overnight that was so frightened by the event that it had to be destroyed. Nobody, thankfully, was reported as being similarly that frightened.

My car was a sorry state, thankfully with the windows intact, but the roof and bonnet looked as if a hammer had been taken to them. A subsequent insurance claim, accompanied by a letter from the mayor and photos from the local newspaper, were accepted. The roof cut off and wing mirrors and the bonnet simply replaced, corrected the damage – all hail to the mighty power of the Almighty.

By midday those billions of wind-heaped hailstones had melted away leaving a distinctly ragged landscape.

10 - Walnut Oil

Enjoying pieces of cooked wild boar occurred in later years when Mme. Gerbeaud invited us to a 'Hunters' Lunch' in a restaurant on the square of the local village of Saint-Vincent-de-Connezac. Lunch was a splendid affair for about twenty-five local farmers, all men, who sat on benches either side of trestle tables. We arrived after everyone had sat down and were found places all together at the end of a bench. We must have looked completely out of place amongst those hard-working men who spent hour after hour in fields under a baking sun. One outstanding unifying feature, apart from their common small stature, was their white foreheads contrasting with their nut-brown faces – the result of always wearing their caps which were now removed for lunch.

I cannot recall the meal in detail other than the main course was boar. It may have actually been the one or a close relative of the fellow that had earlier scared me witless. Either way, it tasted very good, but I was glad it was cooked. Another memory of that meal was the ubiquitous green salad that seemed to be served locally as a mouth cleanser before the dessert courses. The salad was served in a large bowl from which you helped yourself, but once on your own plate the patron drizzled walnut oil over the leaves – delicious and memorable. A great meal finished and we re-entered the blinding sunlight of that small village square to find it filled with people, cars and vans and a strong smell of sunscreen lotion.

I was knocked sideways as I realised it was the preparation of a bike race. Now, bike racing is my game as I had competed as a junior in road and circuit races between the ages of fifteen and eighteen for the Barnet Cycling Club's junior team as a teammate of the great Alfie Engers, known as 'The King'. He became a champion and held countless records and titles, all at national level. Forty-odd years later, I met up with Alfie again – but he never remembered me – that's how memorable my bike riding was.

I have followed continental cycle racing obsessively as a teenager and beyond through the sepia pages of French sports magazines. I'd been visiting France for decades but never understood why I had barely ever seen a racing cyclist even out training, let alone a bike race. Suddenly, I'm in the midst of a French race preparation – joy abounded. The race appeared to be just a local affair with riders from local clubs but the equipment packed into the square in the form of club cars, team vans and sponsored sports vehicles left me speechless compared to what I was used to at home, some twenty-five years earlier – a couple of old vans and maybe a clapped-out car and the riders who had ridden maybe forty miles to the event and the lone, bemused spectator out for a walk with his dog.

We watched the race out on the circuit where I was delighted to understand in my limited French that the 'Break' (the leading group) were already in discussion over dividing up their prize-money –

money they had already won in the intermediate prizes called 'Primes' (eg. first each lap or first over a hill or into a village en route.) What a day – a great meal, with boar and walnut oil, followed by a bike race – that is surely an everyday happening in heaven.

It was later that year I started to read posters which were pasted onto walls or pinned on public noticeboards. They were advertising 'Jours des Fetes' in the surrounding villages and I noticed many included a bike race. Consequently, I began to watch more races. They were the equivalent of the summer village cricket matches in the UK. I even watched a 'Nocturne' – an evening race in Ribérac which was centred around one of the town bars. Now, that's the way to spend an evening!

11 - Eateries

It is difficult – or it certainly was – to get an unenjoyable meal in France but we did experience one in a nearby village, in a restaurant that had changed hands from the previous year. I can't remember the food, other than it was totally unenjoyable, but I do remember one of the constituents – Brussels sprouts. Bloody Brussels sprouts in August, in France, in the Dordogne. Someone was having a laugh.

The mystery was solved when Anita said she heard the new owners speaking English – enough said and certainly enough to never return.

But there were two local outstanding restaurants that we regularly ate at every other evening having eaten in The Hovel on the alternative evenings.

The first was the Hotel De France in Ribérac which we found very early on. The fine 19th-century town-centre hotel was beautifully run by at least three generations of the same family: grandmother, her daughter and her two grandchildren. They opened their restaurant to the public where they served their wonderfully home-cooked food seven days a week. We mostly ate the fixed-price menu which was fixed at a generously low price but high, very high, in value and taste. Three courses for, if I remember correctly, around six pounds.

The main course was invariably corn-fed free-range chicken cooked in butter and served by Madame one-handed with spoon and fork, from a silver dish that was held in the other, with the cooking juices then delicately spooned over the golden offering once on our plates. Accompanying this ambrosial chicken was a dish of real, golden, French fries. Crisp and even and delicious. The other courses were just as exquisite – assiette anglais, charcuterie, pate, the ubiquitous dressed green salad and then the dessert, all accompanied by bread and wine. Bloody wonderful.

The second establishment arrived in the later years and was the local Auberge des Farges – an auberge which was a member of an association of which the members had to self-produce something like 75% of the food served in their dining rooms. Again, so reasonably priced for exquisite home-grown and reared produce. The Auberge itself was a converted cavernous barn with a great fireplace which, when blazing, warmed the great volume on the colder days outside the summer holiday periods. The roof was supported by wonderful, ancient, poplar timber trusses in which, in quieter periods during the meal, one could hear the resident Deathwatch beetles enjoying theirs. The patrons, Jacqui and his wife, ran the place at their own unhurried pace – he was maître d' and waiter and she the chef in the side-annexed kitchen. I recall us having to wait a while between ordering and delivery – but once delivered, what a joy! Home-grown this and home-reared that – soup, rillettes, green-leaf salad, rabbit, chicken, goose, duck, clafoutie – all exquisite and, of course, all accompanied with the wonderful French bread and rustic wine. Both these eateries were worth their weight in gold.

I learnt, much later, of a sinister period in the life of the Hotel de France. It was used as the headquarters of the Gestapo during the latter part of WWII. The local French Resistance, The Marquis, were hiding out in the Foret de Double and causing huge damage to the Nazi infrastructure. In an attempt to stamp this out, Hitler sent troops and the Gestapo to arrest and interrogate the locals. They learnt that local garage owners were supplying petrol to the Marquis and, consequently, four garage owners along with other collaborators were executed. Memorials have been erected in Ribérac to these partisans.

It is difficult to realise that while we had only experienced pleasure in the hotel, some thirty years earlier, others had only experienced unimaginable terror and pain.

The Auberge des Farges, I'm sure, was located in farm buildings on the land of the Château des Farges. This château was razed to the ground and its tenant farmer, in the absence of the owner, was executed when the Gestapo learnt that the Marquis had a base there.

It is difficult to comprehend the complete contrast in the pleasure that we found, with the past horrors of those who suffered at the château and at the Hotel de France, which were unbelievably still within living memory.

12 - Le Moulin

The third eatery was Le Moulin du Roc restaurant. I first learned of this establishment when it was featured in The Sunday Times' colour supplement. The chef patron Madame Gardelou had just been awarded her second Michelin star – the first, I understand from the article, female chef to achieve this accolade. This was obviously an haute cuisine restaurant. The article located Le Moulin near Brantôme at Champagnac-de-Belair, which was virtually on our doorstep. This was the chance I had been waiting for to eat at a fine-dining restaurant as I had always been fearful of such places in the UK – but in France, on holiday, all those class fears evaporated.

I made a decision there and then to eat there.

The intervening year before actually going was one of growing anticipation. All my loose change was hoarded every night in an effort to store cash to allay the cost of such a meal for the four of us: £150-ish was slowly accumulated that year into the meal kitty. The great day eventually arrived with Anita making, days before, the lunchtime reservations over the public phone in the town square in Ribérac. Booted and suited as best we could from the clothes on offer in The Hovel, we arrived. The car parked in their covered, thatched-parking area, we walked down a flower-encrusted path to the entrance. We all felt we had arrived somewhere special and I could feel the tension rising.

Reception accepted our presence and we were shown to our table by an elegant gentleman who we later learnt was Monsieur Gardelou. I had my hand around Jo's neck to frogmarch her forward, as if to the gallows, behind our guide. Anita and Georgia followed behind. Jo subsequently told me the pressure I applied had hurt her neck. This was obviously the result of my inadequacy in the situation and the importance I felt that we all behaved ourselves in such august surroundings and to do nothing out of place on our march to our table in my ridiculous perceived rise in status.

Seated at our white, linen-covered table, adorned with shining, aligned cutlery and sparkling glasses, with assistance from waiters adjusting chairs behind us, we were handed our menus and left to ponder and take in our surroundings. Each table in the restaurant was now occupied, all partially screened by lush, green plants so that a feeling of privacy prevailed. This indeed was a special place. After study, our orders were given and I felt we all began to relax a little. A short time later, classic-looking black and white Parisien-styled waiters towered over us and presented us each with a very small leg of poultry, possibly pigeon, in the middle of an extremely large pure white plate. The origin of the leg was announced but none of my interpreters managed to comprehend its source.

What's this?

We didn't order this! Of course, this is what these fancy sorts of places do – give you unordered food and charge you large extra sums. The magic was dissipating fast. I eventually relaxed by taking the attitude of 'in for a penny in for a pound'. The towering black and white dressed waiters removed the plates, now holding tiny bones. I noticed they rearranged the cutlery in a certain way before lifting the plates.

I cannot now recall the exact contents of the menu or the wine ordered from M.Gardelou who was now acting as the sommelier and said 'Parfait' to my choice even though it was the second cheapest wine on the hugely comprehensive menu. The second cheapest, you note, for I did not want to appear a cheapskate. Bottled water was offered (another ploy to increase the bill), and ordered. Both arrived with a flourish and a sample of the wine poured for tasting. 'Perfect,' I offered in response. The towering waiters appeared again with the starter – probably an exquisite portion of foie gras bloc with accompaniments. This time on completion, to help, I arranged my cutlery in the manner the waiters had previously – only for them to again rearrange this differently before removal. If they were doing this deliberately to make me feel inferior, they were succeeding. The next course, the main, was ceremoniously delivered to the table with each serving beneath a silver-domed salver. Again, announced by another perhaps more senior waiter and, on her signal, the domes were raised simultaneously high above their heads with a great flourish. Of course, this created a special feeling of an event but one of pure pretentiousness – nevertheless, when first experienced, it was splendid theatre. We were all gobsmacked by the procedure. Again, the name of the dish eludes me, but be assured it was superb and not a Brussels sprout in sight!

The game of cutlery positioning would have continued at the completion of this course, but I had decided to give up and let them do their own thing. The next course, the dessert, was remembered and translated as 'A Symphony of Fresh Summer Fruit'. The fruit was covered by a dome of lattice-spun sugar which had to be broken to get to it. All totally exotic to us in those far-off days. Petit fours and coffee completed this exceptional experience, but now the bill had to be paid for. Ten quid a leg, I guessed, making another forty onto the total plus, of course, adding to the service charge. Fearfully, the bill was asked for and when it arrived showed no sign of "legs" and I was not going to raise the matter. The total bill, with the kitty's back-up, came within budget and, feeling even more relaxed, we had a look around the ex-walnut oil mill. What a place – what a setting with thousands of flowers alongside the river Dronne with its clear waters showing off its contented-looking, but always hungry, trout flowing on its way to Ribérac.

Food 10/10; ambience 10/10; service, a bit theatrical but still 10/10. Indeed parfait! At last, I had eaten in a starred restaurant and I was not disappointed in any way. It was not until later we learned that in such upmarket venues 'the legs' constituted an 'amuse bouche' or free 'mouth smiler'. We had much to learn.

The visit to the Moulin became an eagerly awaited ritual each year and very quickly became a totally relaxed experience. Gone were the anxieties of the first visit and we became quite blasé about the whole affair. We even started taking a coffee on the flower-cocooned riverside terrace. Flowers fresh in hue, enchanting the eye and how near the Dronne flows – as Byron (on a bad day) might have put it.

I even ventured a finishing cognac which I ordered from the terrace waiter. Accepting my order, he walked off. Blimey, was he not going to ask me what brand I wanted? He returned with a cognac menu of a hundred or so. The cheapest was around four quid going out to many hundreds a glass. I went to the second cheapest for familiar reasons. This was definitely a style of dining to which we were all complete novices.

In subsequent years, we always lunched with our now l'Audibertian friends Malcolm (he of the septic tank saga) and his wife Peggy. These lunches were always totally enjoyable with all anxieties completely dispersed. Such a lunch followed by a professional bike race would definitely have been heaven.

Mme. Gardelou's reputation had spread worldwide and I understand she was appointed the executive chef for a Presidential Regan/Gorbachev conference banquet in Washington and later the same for the tennis star John "You Cannot Be Serious" McEnroe's wedding breakfast. The funds were obviously coming in and improvements were noticed year on year. A tennis court and a lovely outdoor swimming pool appeared on their land on the opposite side of the Dronne, reached by a delightful pre-rusted arched steel bridge. These excellent facilities were allowed to be used by punters after their lunches. Early on in the years, the classic-dressed towering waiters were replaced by delightful, but lightly trained, young local girls dressed in local costume. The restaurant took a small drop in ambience, but a step up in relaxation.

It remains, decades later, a place I regularly think about and yearn to return to.

13 - Time's Up

There were two great natural events that occurred every August. The first became known to us as the 'Night of the Flying Ants'. This was the evening of the day the female ants, having grown wings, left their nests in their millions to fly off to found new colonies elsewhere. We became aware of this particular day very early on in our tenure when, having eaten out in the evening, we returned to find the bulkhead lamp above the front door – having been left on to lighten our return – had taken on a dull browny/orangey colour. Further inspection found it to be encrusted with thousands of flying ants all fighting to reach the light source as moths to a flame. We soon learnt to enter extremely quickly without turning on any internal lights unless we wanted the house to be invaded by them.

By the following morning, they had all completely disappeared off to their newly created nesting grounds with ample time to establish a safe haven from the slowly encroaching winter.

The second and greater event was the spectacle in Ribérac towards the middle of August of the gathering of hundreds of swallows in the early evenings, hurtling in unison above the streets at roof level, screaming at the top of their voices. I assumed they were that year's youngsters in training for their journey to Africa to spend their first year away from the encroaching European winter. They flew at great speed in a circular movement always following the same route and, from their screams, seemingly thoroughly enjoying themselves.

They always gave me bitter-sweet feeling as I sat at a bar table enjoying my first bevvy of the evening. A few days later, some were to be found resting up on the power cables outside The Hovel – possibly their last resting place before setting off south to Africa. Then, over the next day or so, they were gone taking the glorious high summer with them. This always coincided with the start of our mental preparation for our own journey a few days later the other way, north, to Blighty which in turn brought an end to our high summer.

It was always very noticeable as we headed north that the quality and intensity of daylight started to fade. This was always more evident once we were above the Loire Valley and when the ferry dropped us off in Dover and, with the turning back of the clocks, we immediately lost another hour of the slightly dimmer daylight. The summer holidays had definitely ended and I now felt winter, although still some time off, was definitely lurking.

One compensation on our journey back was the comforting thought that we were carrying Mme. Gerbeaud's yearly present of a tin of her superb homemade foie gras terrine which always memorably kicked off our Christmas day dinner. It was accompanied on one occasion by her own homemade eau de vie which was disguised in a water bottle so as not to contravene our alcohol allowance.

* * *

The years slipped by and Jo and Georgia grew up and became, understandably, more interested in holidays with their friends than with their parents. Anita sought greener pastures and perhaps a better holiday home so 'Les Quatre Murs' became 'Les Trois Murs' and missed its yearly invasion and clean-out.

Eventually deciding to sell, I found myself back in M.Rousillion's bureau to ask for it to be put back on the market. It was a sad trip but it gave me the chance for one final longed for meal at the Auberge des Farge.

"Please wait a minute and Jacqui will join you to go and value your property," said M. Rousillon's successor.

A minute was waited and Jacqui joined me.

"Mon Dieu," I cried when Jacqui appeared. He was the Jacqui, the patron of the Auberge des Farge.

"What's happened to your restaurant?"

"We gave it up as it was too much work."

My little world was dashed as part of my plan was to take the opportunity for that final meal, perhaps as a small sweetener for that bitter decision to sell.

But somehow this incident rounded off and drew a line very neatly under the whole wonderful episode of my venture with France.

I had taken a blind punt on a holiday home in France and at no time had I regretted a single second.

It had been twenty-four years of two and occasional three-week holidays a year which equates roughly to a year in the Dordogne spent for the most part roughly but oh-so-enjoyably.

One of the many, many legacies from that period I am proud of is that both Jo and Georgia from a very early age, have enjoyed a great variety of food – including foie-gras, frog legs, snails, oysters and beyond – and can eat in any restaurant in the world without intimidation.

Merci l'Audibertie. Merci France.

14 - Postscript

I bought The Hovel in 1973. I placed it back on the market around 2003 and sold in 2007. Mark, a young Brit, purchased it as his first permanent home.

He was domiciled in France as a guitar-playing electrician. The price had increased in excess of the purchase price but I doubt it was any more than the inflation. He learnt of the place being for sale through the domiciled artist daughter, and now owner, of the English holiday home that was once the old schoolhouse.

From this chain of events, it can be seen how l'Audibertie was evolving with the second generation of the original holiday-home owners taking over the properties – alongside new owners.

New money was, and is, being pumped in and this can clearly be seen on Google Earth simply by counting the number of swimming pools the hamlet now glories in – eight-ish. When we bought, the only standing water lay in the bottom of deep wells. The coming of mains water to the hamlet was the catalyst for these pools. The mains water arrived in the early eighties when, for some long-forgotten reason, we did not go on holiday that year.

We were therefore not informed of this momentous free event and in the following year were miffed to learn we were the only property to miss out.

To get the installing company to return just for us was going to cost a small fortune, so our old faithful well continued in use.

I've returned to l'Audibertie on three occasions now since ending our holidays. The first was to sign papers at Mark's solicitors for the exchange.

On that trip, I learned that street lighting had arrived in l'Audibertie with The Hovel now boasting a splendid, elaborately curly lamp-bracket fixed on its corner. With these lamps being installed in every hamlet and village in the countryside, the wonderful night viewing of the stars and planets must have dimmed with the resulting light pollution. On that trip I also met up with Amanda, the artist owner of the old schoolhouse, when I enjoyed a splendid alfresco lunch with her and her family. Amanda showed me some of her excellent works, in oils, of local scenes. She sells and teaches art locally.

The second visit was on a trip down to the La Lot area for a holiday with a friend at his friend's lovely, recently built, fully equipped, luxury home. We called, unannounced, into l'Audibertie just to say 'hello' to anyone at home but nobody was – not even Amanda. Unfortunately, I was not able to present her with a fuchsia plant, newly purchased while passing through Ribérac, as a 'thank you' for the previous year's lunch and in return for a hoped-for cup of tea to invigorate us on our onward journey. With no pen and paper to hand to write an accompanying 'thank you' note, I left the plant alone on her doorstep – which must have baffled her on her return.

The third time was with the family – that is Jo, Georgia and her husband Richard and their two splendid daughters, Jessica and Megan. They all stayed in a newly built holiday village just outside

Brantôme, while I stayed in a hotel in the town itself. The plan was to introduce Richard and his girls to the Moulin du Roc, and for me and my girls to eat in the restaurant again.

The Moulin did not disappoint and was everything I was expecting and remembered.

We ate on the awning-shaded terrace alongside the Dronne, surrounded on the other sides by now dense, mature, plants including ten-foot tall bamboo and fruiting banana palms. The food from the set lunch was excellent but the ice cream served with the dessert was decidedly soft – the result of the temperature being in the mid-thirties. Jessica and Megan were not over-impressed with their food as it did not contain sausages or pasta, but they behaved impeccably throughout. A walk around the mill and grounds post-lunch confirmed all our likings of this very special place.

The next day, we all drove to La Jemaye where Jessica and Megan enjoyed the lake as had their mum and aunt years before. The improvements to the facilities at the lake were remarkable with shops, shaded seating areas and even showers installed – not at all like the good old simple days. The journey to the lake that day was broken by another unannounced call into l'Audibertie with the hope of finding Mark in his house but no, he was not at home. A walk around and down memory lane in the High Street, again in blistering 30+ degree heat, showed Jessica and Megan where her immediate family elders had enjoyed previous years. They also learnt of the joys and technique of eating fresh ripe sunflower seeds which I'm sure will be passed on to their future children.

That short break in the Dordogne ended and I returned to Paris for a couple of days with Jo, while the Whitmores headed for the coast.

It was good to see l'Audibertie again and seeing how it had involved from a totally agricultural community to a thriving, holiday, working and prospering hamlet – while still keeping its toe in farming, as well as wonderfully retaining its ancient rural character.

The years have passed since the sale and any contact with the other homeowners I had has now ceased. But Jo and Georgia, particularly Georgia, are still in contact with some of The Kids' Gang members. She even attended one of the gang's wedding. Anita has kept in touch with Malcolm's now sadly widowed wife Peggy.

My only contact during the time the house was on the market was the continued payment of the local taxes and the necessary building insurance.

While these were not huge, they were relentless.

Perhaps the one strong indicator of the joys of L'Audibertie and the region is that a lockateur has returned to buy a holiday home – just like the swallows do.

About the Author

Richard Wall is a north Londoner and qualified as an architect at the Northern Polytechnic, Holloway Road, London, before it became a university of somewhere or other.

He became an amateur Francophile through cycle racing, following the Tour de France and sampling the food when first going abroad to Paris, at the age of 21.

There followed many varied French holidays, including spending a summer as a deckhand on a motor-yacht in the Mediterranean out of Cannes.

Despite failing O-level French, he bought a cottage, as a holiday home, in France.

His main work was in London but he has worked and lived in Bermuda and Dubai.

He now lives back in St Albans after stints in the Isle of Dogs, Hampstead Garden Suburb and Milton Keynes.

He has two daughters and two granddaughters. He wrote and illustrated this account during the Covid lockdowns.

Printed in Great Britain
by Amazon

87374386R00068